MARS, Our Closest Neighbor

by Lucy Williams Jackson

HOUGHTON MIFFLIN BOSTON

Contents

The Red Planet 3

The First Missions 6

Spirit and *Opportunity* 8

The NASA Science Team 13

Success for the Rovers..........15

Mars Facts............................16

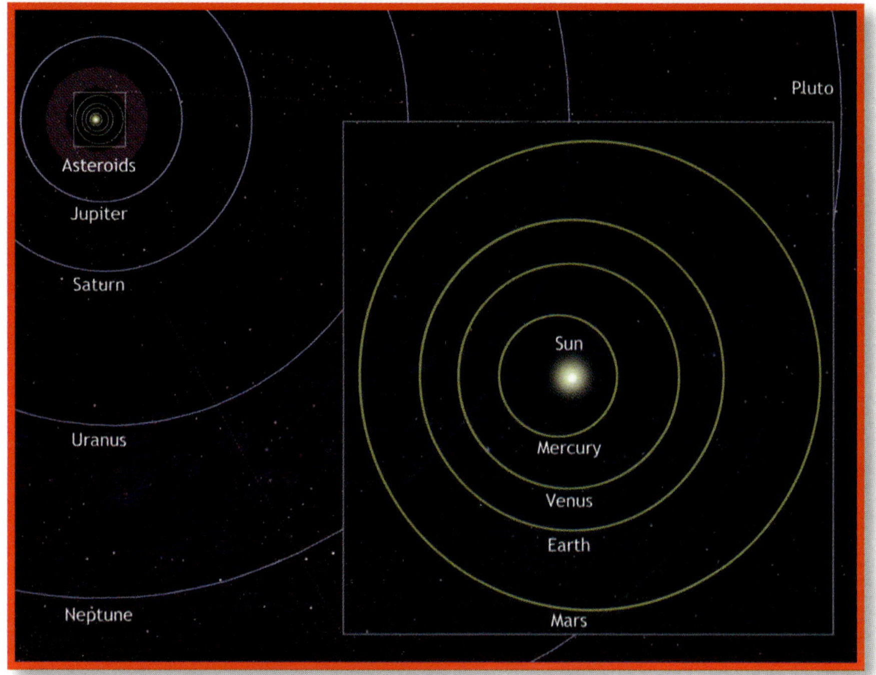

Mars is the fourth planet from the Sun.

The Red Planet

Look up at the stars on a clear night. There's one bright red light in the sky. That's not a star—it's the "red planet" Mars, the fourth planet from the Sun. Of all the planets, it's the one closest to Earth.

Mars is fascinating to people. Scientists think that this cold, dry planet might have once been warm and wet. They also think that humans could someday live on Mars. Let's find out what scientists are doing to learn more about Mars, our closest neighbor.

Mars is similar to Earth, yet different, too. It has about the same land area as Earth. It has a moon—actually two moons, Phobos and Deimos. They are both a lot smaller than Earth's Moon.

The temperature varies on Mars. Daytime near its equator is around 80° F (27° C). That's the temperature of a summer day on Earth. A night at one of its poles can dip to an incredibly cold -200° F (-129° C).

Mars has a thin atmosphere made mostly of carbon dioxide gas, so humans would not be able to breathe there. Plus, the pull of it's gravity isn't as strong as the gravity on Earth. Instead of walking, you'd bounce to school!

There are polar ice caps on Mars. Scientists know that there are large amounts of frozen water in these ice caps. Scientists think that Mars was different a long time ago. Landforms reveal that liquid water once flowed there. Certain markings show that there were once streams on the ground.

Mars has dust storms with different levels of intensity.

The First Missions

Many years ago, scientists started looking into the sky to find out more about the mysterious Mars. Earth telescopes couldn't get a close enough view. Then scientists began building flyby spacecraft. As their name states, they flew by and took pictures of our neighbor planet.

In 1960, the former Soviet Union sent *Marsnik 1* and *Marsnik 2* to bring back information about the space between Earth and Mars and about the surface of Mars. *Marsnik 1* and *Marsnik 2* never made it. The spacecraft didn't have enough power to leave Earth's atmosphere.

The United States sent the first successful mission to Mars. *Mariner 4* flew by the "red planet" in July 1965. It brought back 21 close-up pictures of the surface. The pictures revealed that Mars was barren. It had no plant life. It did have many big holes called craters.

The data from the *Mariner 4* mission also revealed that the atmosphere on Mars was made up of carbon dioxide. Before this, scientists believed the Martian atmosphere contained oxygen, similar to Earth's.

Mariner 1 **was launched in 1962. It did not make it to Mars.**

For more than 40 years, there have been many missions to Mars. About a dozen have been successful. The data from those missions continue to give scientists important information. The newest missions will tell even more.

Spirit and *Opportunity*

The National Aeronautics and Space Administration (NASA) created two robot-like vehicles to roam Mars. They are called Mars Exploration Rovers (MERs). *Spirit* and *Opportunity* launched from rockets from Cape Canaveral, Florida, in 2003. *Spirit* launched on June 10, and *Opportunity* launched on July 7. They both entered the Martian atmosphere several months later.

Their landings on Mars were spectacular. Both landed with the help of parachutes. Their fall was cushioned by inflated airbags that surrounded them. When landing, each rover bounced about a dozen times. The first bounce reached more than 100 feet (30 m) into the air!

The air went out of the airbags, and out rolled the tightly folded and protected MERs. Each was about 380 pounds (172 kg). They were expected to travel about 100 yards (91 m) every Martian day, or so.

Spirit landed at Gusev Crater. Scientists believe that this crater was formed when a meteor struck the planet a long time ago. *Spirit* landed in a basin that was possibly once filled with water.

A mission to Mars could look something like this.

Opportunity landed at Meridiani Planum, on the opposite side of Mars. By a stroke of good luck, it landed in a crater that contained exposed bedrock—the first ever seen on another planet. Scientists think that bedrock reveals more about past environment than loose rocks or boulders that might have come from somewhere else.

Beginning their journeys, each MER took a panorama, a continuous photograph of the land surrounding them. Special images revealed the best route to travel, and that's where they headed.

Spirit and *Opportunity* had cameras attached above them to give scientists human-like views of the land. When the MER reached a target, the robotic arm—complete with elbow and fist—put a scientific instrument up against it to view it and record the data.

The MER was equipped with instruments to collect the data. Magnets attracted dust particles. A special X-ray analyzed the makeup of the rocks, soils, and dust. The Rock Abrasion Tool, or RAT, acted like a rock hammer. It broke open weathered rock to expose the insides for study.

During its journey of Gusev Crater, *Spirit* found a rock. The scientists called it Mazatzal. It had two hints that water might have washed upon it in the distant past: the scallop shapes on its surface and bright mineral lines inside it. Mazatzal was a great find for *Spirit* geologists, the scientists who study rocks and soil.

This is a computer-generated illustration of a Mars Exploration Rover.

Opportunity stayed in Eagle Crater for two months. Eagle was the 70-foot-wide (21 m) crater it had landed in. Driving was dangerous at times. Navigating high cliffs, the Earth drivers knew that one wrong move could send *Opportunity* falling. They determined that the crater's bedrock looked like meteorites found on Earth that scientists had believed had come from Mars.

Opportunity found round blue pebbles in a hole nicknamed the Berry Bowl. A mineral found on the "blueberries" typically forms from being in water. This was another sign that water once existed on Mars.

The *Opportunity* scientists were fascinated by Wopmay, a lumpy boulder inside another crater called Endurance Crater. Not able to get close enough to touch, *Opportunity* took photos of an interesting area called Burns Cliff.

These NASA scientists are part of the MER team.

The NASA Science Team

A talented group of scientists was behind the MER project. From information gathered from past missions to Mars, the team selected the two destinations, Gustev Crater for *Spirit* and Meridiani Planum for *Opportunity*. Data revealed that these places once had water.

Now the big task: Navigators at the NASA Jet Propulsion Laboratory worked for three years to plan a trajectory, or course, to get the rovers to these locations. Do you think it's hard to hit the center of a far-off target? The navigators had to calculate the exact speed of a rotating Earth, a rotating Mars, and a rotating spacecraft while all were orbiting the Sun over months of travel time and 300 million miles (483 million km) of distance to land precisely at these areas. Bull's-eye! They did it.

Navigators did an amazing job, and so did the spacecraft design team. *Spirit*'s spacecraft was "quiet." That means it moved very predictably throughout the flight to Mars so adjustments could be made to keep it on course. When entering the Martian atmosphere, it was only about a half-mile off course.

Once the rovers landed on Mars, the geologists took over. They worked hard to gather the data from the rocks and soil. While they were looking down, an atmospheric team looked up. These scientists noted the light, weather patterns, and dust accumulation.

Could humans live on Mars? We'll know someday, thanks to *Spirit* and *Opportunity* and science teams that continue to study Mars data.

Success for the Rovers

The *Spirit* and *Opportunity* missions were extremely successful. The rovers lasted for many months longer than ever imagined. They gathered information that will be useful for years.

There are several more missions planned for the next decade. As early as 2011, NASA plans a "sample return" mission. Pieces of the Martian land will be brought back to Earth for examination.

The journeys of *Spirit* and *Opportunity* will be long remembered. Scientists even named two asteroids after them, which is a great honor. That isn't bad for two dirt-digging robots roaming around Mars.

A RAT arm helps collect data from the surface of Mars.

Mars Facts

- Fourth planet from the Sun, the next beyond Earth
- Distance from Earth: 249 million to 339 million miles (400 million km to 545 million km)
- Two moons: Phobos and Deimos
- Revolves around the Sun once every 687 Earth days
- Gravity only 38 percent as strong as Earth's
- Length of day: 24 hours, 39 minutes, 35 seconds
- Atmosphere is mostly carbon dioxide (95.3 percent)
- Winds up to 80 miles (128 km) an hour
- Temperatures range range from -99° F (-73° C) during polar night to 80° F (27° C) at Martian equator during midday